My Grandma

Mama

The Family

Our House in Scranton

My Sister at Christmas

Me

BEEN TO YESTERDAYS

Poems of a Life
by LEE BENNETT HOPKINS

Illustrations by CHARLENE RENDEIRO

Wordsong/Boyds Mills Press

Published by Wordsong
Boyds Mills Press, Inc.
A Highlights Company
815 Church Street
Honesdale, Pennsylvania 18431
Printed in China

Publisher Cataloging-in-Publication data
Hopkins, Lee Bennett.
   Been to yesterdays : poems of a life / by
Lee bennett Hopkins ; illustrations by
Charlene Rendeiro.— 1st ed.
[64]p. : ill. ;   cm.
Includes index.
Summary : Autobiographical poems capture a
thirteen-year-old boy's feelings, experiences,
and aspirations in one tumultuous year of
his life.
ISBN 1-56397-467-3 (hc.)
ISBN 1-56397-808-3 (pbk.)
1. Poets, American—20th century—Juvenile
biography. 2. Youth—Biography—Juvenile
poetry. 3. Hopkins, Lee Bennett.
[1. Poets, American. 2. Youth—Poetry.
3. Hopkins, Lee Bennett.] I. Rendeiro,
Charlene, ill. II. Title.
811.54—dc20   1995   CIP   AC
94-73320

First edition, 1995
First Boyds Mills Press paperback edition, 1999
Book designed by Jean Krulis
The text of this book is set in
13-point Usherwood Medium.

  (hc) 10 9 8 7 6 5
(pbk) 10 9 8 7 6 5 4 3 2 1

To four unique Mothers—

    Elizabeth M. Brown (for memories)

    Bernice E. Cullinan (for tomorrows)

    Elizabeth Isele (for "yesterdays")

    and my own (for always)

—L.B.H.

"SMILE

for the camera,"
the photographer
said
as we posed,
all dressed up
in our best
Sunday clothes.

"Smile big now.
Smile wide.
The five of you
look like
birds of a feather
nestled
together."

Daddy held Mama
tenderly,
juggled
my baby sister
on his knee.

Daddy.
Mama.
Sister.
Brother.
Me.

The
five of us—
smiling
for the camera,
blessed
as could be—

The five of us—

A
picture-perfect
family.

PACK

the boxes
into the car,
pile the dishes,
load in the clothes,
squeeze in the
pots and pans,
our two radios—
can't waste a space—
everything goes.

Crowd in the Mama,
the Daddy,
the sister,
jam in the brother,
make room for my toes—
can't waste a space—
everything goes.

Bundle the memories
we're moving today
from
Scranton, PA,
to
Newark, NJ.

RIDING

and
riding
miles
upon
miles

moves us
nearer to Newark

toward
Grandma's
warm
smiles.

WOOLWORTH:
DOWNTOWN NEWARK

was the biggest store
I had ever seen
ever been to
in my entire life.

Its
aisle after aisle
seemed
to cover
mile after mile
of pile after pile
of the most
fascinating things—

hinges and springs,
rubber bands, rings,
teddy bears, chairs,
wax apples and pears,
wooden hangers for clothes,
fish—

"And look at this
butter dish,"
Mama said
with a big, wide grin.

"This is what
rich people
put their butter in."

Our butter
was always
set upon the table
in its see-through
cellophane.

Plain.

"How much is it?"
I asked.

"Twenty-nine cents.
Can you imagine?
Twenty-nine cents!
It don't make sense,"
Mama said.

Someday
we'll be rich
I thought.

Rich enough
to own
a dish
like that.

I knew
if I saved enough
hard enough
long enough
that this
twenty-nine-cent
butter dish
would be
a wish
come true.

My present
to Mama
for Christmas
this year.

A Christmas surprise.
A butter-dish-fuss.

A rich dish
for a
rich family—

A
family
like
us.

CLUTCHING

her
small
son's
hand,
a lady
smiled at me
and said
to Mama:

"What a good lookin'
young 'un you got there.
What bright-eyed eyes.
What sleek brown hair.
Why
God must've
given them
special on him.

"Hymns
from
Him."

Mama didn't answer.
She didn't return
the lady's kind smile.

She tugged me away
down the toy aisle.

"Their skin's
so dark,"
I said.

"They're niggers,"
Mama answered.
"That's what they're called.
You'll see
a lot
of niggers
here in this town."

Niggers.

It didn't sound
so good
when Mama said it—
when the lady's smile
disappeared—
turned
a sadlike frown.

Her face
showed
a sadness
of a kind
I just couldn't
seem to erase
from my mind.

That afternoon
alone with Grandma
I told her
I saw two niggers.

"Where?
When?"
she asked.

"This afternoon
when Mama
took me to
Woolworth's
five-and-ten."

"Nigger's not
a good word
to choose.
Call them
coloreds.
Coloreds
is a better word
to use.

"Words
can be tricky.
Some words
can hurt
when you
blurt 'em out.
Cause
undue sorrow.
Cause
undue pain.
Don't go
usin' that
word again."

I thought
about what
Grandma said
all night long
as I lay
in bed—

the word

niggers

bounced
through
my brain—
sped
through
my
head.

I learned
a lesson
from Grandma
about words
today—

that
some words
are right
some are
too strong

still others—

terribly
wrong.

THERE

are
things
you feel
inside—

things
you cannot
always
hide—

things
you wish
you never
knew—

things
you pray
just won't
come true.

I know
that
something's
going on.

I don't know
what it is
or why

but

this morning
in the kitchen
when I saw
Mama cry
all day long
her hurt
went
through
my
mind—

a kind
of pain
I could not
leave
behind.

Something
wrong is
happening.

An aching
burning
something-thing.

I don't know
what it is
or why—

it
won't
leave me alone
no matter
how
I
try.

ANOTHER

long
drawn-out
night

another
bitter, brutal
fight.

Time
stood still
till
morning
broke
with a
trembling
throbbing
terrored-force—

as
I woke up
sleepily
half-believing

I hadn't
heard
the
dreaded
word—

divorce.

WHEN

Daddy
slammed shut
the
front-room door
five
minus one
left
only four.

As
a branch
was slashed
from our
family tree
I wondered
how
this
could have
come to be.

WHEN

Daddy
left us,
he left his
bedroom slippers
beneath the sink
on the bathroom floor.

When
Mama put them
in the giveaway bag
for the poor,
I knew
this time
Daddy
had gone
out the door
for good.

I never
understood
why
he went away
but
every
night
I pray

that
the daddy
who gets
to wear
his slippers
will be kinder
to his family
than Daddy
was to us—

to me.

He has to be.

He
has
to
be.

"SINCE

your
sister's asleep
and your brother
is too,
there are
some things
I must say to you
'cause
you're the oldest,
strongest,
my number one son.

"Someday
you will understand
that life can't flow
as you always planned.

"Your Daddy and I
don't see eye to eye,
can't get along,
anymore—
I don't even
know why.

"But he's still
your Daddy.
He always will be.
He's still a good man.
Still part of me.

"It's important to know
that he'll always
love you,
your sister,
your brother,
and Grandma too.

"Although we're
going to be apart
he'll always love you
with all his heart.

"That's all I have
 to tell you now.

"I know Daddy's leaving
 is hard to bear.

"The four of us
 will have to fare—

"no matter
 what
 no matter
 where."

JUST

when
everything
seems
to go
along
just
fine

Life
comes by
and
throws
you
its
line.

"WE

have to
move again
tonight.
Mama's money's
spent.
I don't have
enough
to make
our monthly rent.
The check
that Daddy said
he'd send
was never sent."

Again
I look
at empty boxes
and know
what they
are for.

They're
made
to store
some things
you live
your whole life
for—

a teddy bear,
books,
old door keys,
silent
lasting
memories.

Stowed in cardboard
corners,
memories rest

quietly

in paper chests

there—

when you need
them most
to move you on—

there—

when we must
take flight
in the middle
of a
wrinkled,
corrugated
night.

SO

we
climb
another
wobbly
staircase
into
another
hollow
place.

So
we
climb
to the
top floor
stair-after-stair
where
a
bare
room
anxiously
stares
at us
there.

MAMA,

looking
tired,
weary,
said,

"Son,
I don't
like that
dreary frown
perched
on your face.

"I know
what's on
your mind.
I know
your *every* look.
I know you
like a book.

"Right now
　this dreary place
　don't look like much,
　but it will
　when I give it
　your Mama's
　touch.

"I'll find
　the means
　to fix up
　this place.

"I'll put curtains
　on these windows.
　Saw some
　down in
　Woolworth's,
　fine ones
　starched and stiff
　made of
　fancy, frilly lace.

"I'll paint
this apartment
head to toe—
the ceilings,
the walls,
the halls.
These rooms'll glow.
This will all be
spanking new
when I get through.
Won't take
no time
for me to do.
No time at all.

"Things'll get better.
I'll make them so.
You'll see.
Have faith in your Mama.
Believe in me.

"Get some sleep now.
It's been a rough day.
Think what
tomorrows
will bring our way."

"'Night, Mama,"
I said
as I went off to bed,
looking again
at the room's
empty space
and the
smile-through-a-frown look
on
Mama's
worn
face.

"UNCLE

John"
and
"Uncle Ron"
and
"Uncle Chad"
and
"Uncle Brad"—

One of
these days
maybe
one of these
"uncles"
will become
a real
dad.

STARING

out
the window
on the long ride
to
South Eighth Street School
on the
bursting
crowded
city bus

I wonder
if Daddy
ever—

even for a
little while—

thinks
about me—

thinks
about
us.

WE

played
baseball
every spring.

He taught me
every single thing
I had
to know—

how to bat
to bunt
to throw.

But
since
he went away
that day
the game
will never
be the same.

The bleachers,
the bases,
the catcher's mitt
seem
empty

barren
now

like me

deserted
lonely
a
"Strike-three-
        OUT!"

And
I realize
what
losing
is
all
about.

GRADES

K through three
in Scranton, PA.

Grade four
in
faraway
Newark, NJ.

Grade five
another school
another teacher
another new face.

Grade six
in some other
new part
of another
Newark-place.

One thing
I learned
from all
of these
schools

is that
I
am someone
who will
make
my
own
rules.

"WHAT

do you
want to be
when you grow up?"
asked my teacher,
Miss Ethel K. Tway.

Down the rows
the kids called out:

    "A cop."
    "A nurse."
    "A soldier."
    "A sailor."
    "A scientist."
    "Butcher!"
    "A firefighter."

When she got to me
I said,

    "A writer."

Louis laughed
hysterically.

"A *writer*!"
he said.
"What a crazy thing
to want to be!"

"I don't think
that's funny, Louis,"
said Miss Tway.
"Everyone's entitled
to sound
their own voice.
Becoming
a writer is a
fine life-choice."

That special moment
on that
red-letter day
I fell madly
in love
with
Miss Ethel K. Tway.

STILL

there

on your chair
my
one-eyed
tattered
teddy bear.

Still
there

on your chair

the book
you were reading
that night
to me

the bookmark
still tucked
to
page thirty-three.

Still
there

on your chair
your knitting needles
berry-blue—

a half-made
mitten
for
me
from you.

Your chair
is still—
but
it's still there.

Your pillow
smells
of
perfumed hair.

I *see*
your smile.

I *feel*
your touch.

I miss you so
so
so
so
much.

I miss you
morning,
noon,
and night.

I love you,
Grandma.

Good-bye.

Sleep tight.

WHEN

Grandma
read me:

> *Humpty Dumpty*
> *Sat on a wall.*
> *Humpty Dumpty*
> *Had a great fall . . .*

I never
knew
that
Humpty's
fall
was
something
that
someday
comes
to
us
all.

CHRISTMAS

is here—

night's
crispy-clear—

tinsel
is hung—

paper chains
strung—

on
top of the tree
sits
a
shimmering
star—

if only
Mama
would
come home
early tonight
from

      MARY'S INN

the
just-around-the-corner
neighborhood
bar.

"ONE HUNDRED

bottles of beer on the wall.
One hundred bottles of beer.
If one of the bottles
happened to fall—
ninety-nine bottles of beer
on the wall.

"Ninety-nine
bottles of beer on the wall.
Ninety-nine bottles of beer . . ."

If only
all
the
bottles of beer
could
somehow
right now
suddenly
disappear.

UNDERNEATH

our
Christmas tree
is the box
I wrapped
in white

with a big
gold bow
on top of it
to make it
shiny bright.

Inside the box
is Mama's gift
with a note
I wrote
that says:

"This gift
is special, Mama,
just for you.
I hope
you'll like this
butter dish."

A
secret
Woolworth-wish
I made
last summer
did come
Christmas-true.

WHEN

I was young,
before
I went
to bed,
a nursery rhyme
that Grandma
read
each night
still
echoes
through
my head:

When I was just a little he,
My Grandma took me on her knee.
Her smiles and kisses gave me joy
Each time she called me "Darling Boy."

But
now
there's
no more
little he

no more
sitting on
Grandma's knee

no more
smiles
or kisses
or joy

no more
darling

no more
boy.

BEEN

to
yesterdays.

Lived
through
todays.

Looking on
toward
tomorrows—

new characters,
new plays.

The whys
of life
change

so
do
ways

new scenery
is built
to fill
an empty stage.

Tomorrow
I turn
thirteen.

The calendar
turns
a page:

      Come-along-
        a-fresh-new-day.
      Come-along-
        new-age.

DEAR

Lord—

Please
give me
the strength
to try

the strength
to laugh
the strength
to cry

the strength
to hope
the strength
to cope

the strength
to one day
say good-bye
to fly
into
a
brighter
sky.

It's good
to know
You're
always there—

that
I can
share with You
this prayer.

Thank You
for listening
once again.

Good night
Dear Lord,

Amen.

      Amen.

TO

make
this world
a whole lot
brighter

when
I
grow up
I'll
be
a writer.
I'll
write about
some things
I know—

>   *how to bunt*
>   *how to throw . . .*
>
>   *a Christmas wish*
>   *a butter dish . . .*
>
>   *a teddy bear*
>   *an empty chair . . .*

the love I have inside
to
share . . .

Yes.

To
make
this world
a whole lot
brighter,

when
I grow up
I'll
be
a
writer.

INDEX OF TITLES

My Grandma

Mama

The Family

Our House in Scranton

My Sister at Christmas

Me